Realities of Life

Also by Donald W. Grant

Poetry

Shades of Life
Echoes of Life
Silence of Life
Reflections of Life
Trials of Life
Ecstasy of Life

Essays

M.A.G.A.: Making America Go Awry

Realities of
Life

A Collection of Poems

By
Donald W. Grant

DC
D2C Perspectives

Contents

An Omen

We have all seen rainbows in the sky,
the multicolored magic of moisture and light
arched from horizon to horizon, always
making us think for a moment of a pot of gold.

At times, there may only be part of an arch,
an arc of brilliant colors falling from the sky.
Other times, on that rare occasion, a full circle.

But once, I saw a rainbow lying parallel
along the base of the mountains as if
it had grown tired and needed to rest.

Was this an omen, a glimpse into my future?
Was the universe sending me a message?

This may have been the day I decided
I too needed to rest, for shortly after
I quit my job to be a full-time poet.

Deflection

The body knows no difference
between good and bad stress

Whether we feel elation or depression
the body could care less

Tension, frustration, anger
all emotions our mind rejects

Transforming them into pain
be at back, shoulder, or neck

The mind protecting itself
deflecting to others the blame

That we go along with this,
accept it, is really a shame

So much of our brain
we do not understand

We can probe and prod
but it stays in command

Hiding the power, it could yield
protecting itself from all damage

If we could ever unlock its secrets
maybe we would be more than

just God's image.

Misjudged

She sat on the couch with a look of despair
as if the burdens of the world were upon her
shoulders

Was it the frustration of the pandemic,
the loss of control over her environment?

Was it the pressure of deadlines and ideas,
so much to accomplish in so short a time?

Was it the lunacy of the current political climate,
the stupidity of people still following an imbecile?

As I watched her, my mind tried to think of fixes,
how or what could I say to raise her spirits.

I quietly asked, "Why the look of despair?"
She looked up and said, "Oh, I was just thinking
about getting tacos for dinner."

A Villanelle for Lexus

They began with the theory of Kaizen
doing something no one thought they could
making the best of luxury sedans.

Taking small steps to get the upper hand
knowing full well just where they stood
they began with the theory of Kaizen

They knew success would create a demand
with the finest of engineers and plans they would
be making the best of luxury sedans

Success realized, they had taken command
others now were asking should
they began with the theory of Kaizen

Sadly, number one status would not stand
new faces emerged who never understood
making the best of luxury sedans

New faces not taught the theory of Kaizen
letting customer service slip ever backward
forgetting they began with the theory of Kaizen
making the best of luxury sedans.

Dissonance

A butterfly flaps its wings
A hurricane ravishes the coast

An old man yells at children on his lawn
A baby falls asleep to the sound of a lullaby

The wind is piling trash in an alley
The tide is smoothing the sand along the beach

A mother kisses the bruise on her child's arm
A wife attempts to cover her bruise with makeup

A bird soars high above the treetops
A man leaps from a bridge in despair

Rain pounds, rivers overflow, towns flood
A child runs, leaps into the backyard pool

Smoke belches from the refinery nearby
The aroma of BBQ entices the neighbors

Horns blowing, engines revving, drivers screaming
In the forest, serenity, quiet, all is still

Hearts filled with hate covered in hoods
Arms embracing, the power of love released

Humanity at a crossroads
One path effulgent

The other leading to dissonance

A People's Pantoum

There are two kinds of people in the world
those who talk and those who listen.
This applies to both boys and girls
or should I correctly say men and women?

Of those who talk and those who listen
one is self-centered the other empathetic.
Again, they can be either men or women.
One who talks and never listens is pathetic

If one's self-centered and not empathetic
they miss most of life, which is sad,
for one who talks and never listens is pathetic
often causing a good relationship to go bad.

One missing most of life, which is sad,
talking over people, not paying attention
causes a good relationship to go bad
which I'm sure was not their intention

Talking over people, not paying attention
is just the opposite of those who listen,
which I'm sure was not their intention
but a trait no one wants to mention

And is just the opposite of those who listen
this applies to both boys and girls,
and as a trait no one wants to mention,
Explains why there are two kinds
of people in the world

Sonnet XCVI

Stormy Night

The quiet of the night disturbed by thunder
preceded by rain and flashes of lightning.
The rumble and explosions ever so frightening,
our cats trembling, afraid, scurrying to go under

the covers with us, where they feel safe and sound
bursts of noise, rain, and flashes of light
continue until the sun breaks replacing the night
and now all is quiet, and our cats are nowhere to be
found.

While the day brings blue skies, the wind fresh air
we are trying to recover from our lack of sleep
and although the storm is just about to disappear
the intense heat of summer is woefully still here

the smell of fresh rain when we breath in real deep
and the white clouds, make up, almost, for our lack
of sleep

Shark!!

The bay in the early morning
When the tide is low, resembles
A lake more than the ocean
As water gently laps upon the shore

The surface shimmering glass-like
Broken occasionally by a cormorant
Seeking their morning sustenance

Below the surface sharks glide undetected
Their presence only revealed by the sign
As you enter the beach, warning you
To swim at your own risk!

Today a new sign has appeared
Warning of an aggressive shark.
Is that not an oxymoron?
Are not all sharks aggressive?
Is that not the nature of a shark?

We never see a fin skimming along
Nor a shark leaping into the air
But just knowing they are out there
Keeps us walking along the shore with care!

An Evangelical Sestina

Fortunately, there are less and less evangelicals
which means less and less hypocrites
standing supposedly above us on the Bible
trying to convince us they are followers of Christ
when it's easier to say they are closer to the devil
finding themselves rejected by God and on the road
to hell.

They want to say it is we who are going to hell
for supporting Biden, not Trump as evangelicals
are doing which makes them even more hypocritical.
They back a man who has never read the Bible,
who feels he is number one above even Christ,
when we all know he is more like the devil.

The so called pastor, Robert Jeffries, like the devil
himself, who said there is no chance in hell
that Biden would ever get the vote of evangelicals
and those that do are the biggest of hypocrites
because he favors abortion which in the Bible
is an abomination in the eyes of Christ

Jeffries is mistaken as abortion is not a word Christ
ever used, nor can a Christian ever be condemned
by the devil and face the fiery furnaces of hell.
He is forgetting that he and other evangelicals
Are the modern Pharisees, the hypocrites

That brought the seven woes in the Bible.

It was the Pharisees who according to the Bible
caused the anger and cursing of Christ
as he called them vipers and of the devil
who may never see heaven but hell,
where all the so-called evangelicals
will be tossed along with the other hypocrites.

Sinners were forgiven but never hypocrites
As they at least according to the Bible
Kept people from accepting Christ
And as sly and slick as the devil
Blocked the path to heaven leaving hell
The only choice left like the pseudo evangelicals.

According to the Bible, the only time Christ lost
his temper was when the hypocrites, like the modern
evangelicals, steered people to hell.

Inferno

The sun is a red ball in the sky
ash is covering everything my eye
can see, and smoke
blots the sky no longer blue

When lightning struck and thunder clapped
a few days ago, we thought perhaps
there might be a fire or two if that,
but over three hundred! Can that be true?

Two fires alone causing mass evacuation
now merged into one causing more devastation,
acres in flames more ruination
As we sit here, what are we to do?

The smell of smoke fills the air
making it hard to breathe and there
is only one road out of here
So here we sit, our cats and just us two.

No Angel

In his Ode *To The West Wind*
Shelley penned the line
"Angels of rain and lightning."

Sitting now surrounded by smoke and fire
air no human should have to breathe
'twas no angel that caused this frightening

inferno that only a demon from Hell
could conceive, causing destruction
by fire and wind and ash raining

down on forests and towns
scorching the earth and structures
as animals and people are fleeing

No angel would cause this devastation
turning Nature's beauty to ash and rubble
thousands displaced, only thing left is praying.

A Wonder

Life begins with us
not knowing how to love
or how to hate

Unfortunately, these are things
we learn from those around
us whom we imitate

Watching a small child repeat
what we say or act out in
a certain way is usually great

until they do or say something
they should not then we
realize it is too late

As we look back at the
choices we have made,
some good, some we hate

we try to pass them along
to those coming behind
if only we could communicate

We forget those before us
tried to share with us but
we thought they were out of date

So this vicious circle repeats
and I often wonder what will it take
for humanity to finally escape

And just get along.

A Feline Ballad

They started out life abandoned
six little kittens lying side by side
placed in a box and left out stranded
four adopted, two by us, sadly, two died

We named one Cleopatra the other Isis
the Queen of Egypt and Goddess of Fertility
both full of life and abundant cuteness
like any two sisters, different personalities

Cleo is more nervous, maybe a bit shyer
Isis is more cuddly, always needing a lap
Cleo eats last, respecting her sister
both spend their day mostly taking naps

They hate when we leave, wanting us to stay
even though the woman who comes by
and watches them while we are away
treats them well, they still like to cry

as we go out the door, they make us feel guilty
sad little faces as if again being abandoned
they should know by now in reality
we would never ever leave them stranded.

America Revisited

Thank you Allen Ginsberg
your voice has been heard
and the baton has been passed on.
Willingly, I take up where
you left off, although nothing
has really changed here, in America.

Who would have thought when
she was in her infancy that
this republic would be on the brink
of losing its democracy.
The vision of its creators
on the verge of being a nightmare.
Where does one begin to describe
the erosion of a nation in disarray?
We thought we had progressed.
we believed we had evolved,
in truth we were blind, we digressed.
now with even more issues to solve.

Black lives matter may be the spark
that awakens the nation from its apathy.
All men have not been allowed to be equal.
We fooled ourselves by attaching new labels,
no longer nigger, no longer colored, but black
yet the suppression remains, subtle but intact.
Our streets now filled with those who refuse

to settle for the status quo,
protesting that now is the time
for hatred and bigotry to go.

The bomb you so eloquently told
to go fuck itself is no longer a threat
and our battle with Russia no longer cold.
They have invaded without a shot
and disrupted from within with weapons
of division and doubt.

Time magazine is a relic of the past
replaced by Facebook and Twitter,
emotions now expressed in feeds and bytes.
Debate replaced by opinions and hate.
You could now be president
being Catholic no longer a barrier,
others have set that precedent
though they were killed, which is scarier.
But you would be free to smoke
as that restriction has been lifted
marijuana now legal, so you can stoke
letting your mind be totally drifted.

Our eggs are still in our basket
as India starves, our nest well-stocked
the world no longer respects us
our borders locked and president mocked.

The flag you remember of red, white and blue
no longer a symbol of freedom and hope

now flown to exclaim isolationism here
love it or leave it and pass me a beer.

The daily grind of nine to five you railed against
replaced by twelve-hour days and vacationless years
technology our master, progress the gears
that keep us enslaved.

So while you have been laid to rest
shoulder no longer at the wheel
those of us who are still left
with issues you could not imagine
(climate change, pandemic, gutless politicians)
are trying to carry on as if
the destruction of this world were no big deal.

The Grifters

Supposedly, they came from New Jersey
across the country in an RV
Landing in our little town
on a street not too far from me.

The RV sat out front and with an apology
the grifter started his diatribes publicly
using the Nextdoor app to let the neighbors
know the things he needed for his family.

Now in an empty house they needed cutlery,
furniture, dishes, bedding and anything free
even a used truck for a business he
hoped to start to support his family.

He had a wife, sons to the count of three,
a deck cleaning business that he hoped would be
the revenue source to meet all their needs
at least, that is what he led us to believe.

He said he had a visitation by an angel, so heavenly.
She said all will be well, all will be hunky-dory.
He took this as a sign to add to his talents
so he took up painting as his next hobby

He used Nextdoor to display his artistry
Sadly, it looked more like a child at play

Whether he sold any I do not know
but he saw this as a way to make more money.

Next they surprised us they were moving away
their rental for sale, they could not stay
The owner gave them ninety days to move
A standard amount by landlords today

Then they announced a catastrophe
they were being evicted, how could this be
People had forgotten the notice before
and so, the neighbors poured out their sympathy.

But they found a farm where their dogs could play
Just down the road, a few miles away
but the truck they had been given no longer ran
so they moved all but it, for someone else to tow
away.

Things were quiet until one day
they announced they had a huge bill to pay
just before Christmas they used too much heat
Four-thousand dollars they now owed to PG&E

Once again, the neighbors rose to save the day
Donating funds to keep the creditors at bay
Next they announced they had a room to spare
and they were looking for someone to share and pay.

From time to time they had good things to say
How great God had been and that they could pray

for the world to be a better place, for all to get along
after all they had been blessed up to this day.

Then one night, lightning and thunder came our way
Fires were in the mountains, people told not to stay
thousands evacuated as the blaze took its toll
and up popped the Grifters, a new scam to play

They said they had found a place to stay
having been evacuated from Felton and got away
just in time ahead of the fire, and were now
sheltering at the Seascape Resort,
a very pricey place to stay.

Now they needed clothing, food, and of course
money, but this time they had a son and daughter
with them to stay and at least two dogs who did not
get along so any help would be great so they could
be okay

As if all this was not enough, they had more to say
He now was an ordained minister and not only
could pray but wanted to start his own church which
we all know would just be another way to get the
suckers to pay.

This is not the end of my little tale
for who knows what they will do next
all I know for sure is when they die
heaven will be closed, welcome to hell.

Writers Against Trump

Voices not usually heard
uniting to spread the word

Those who normally have pen in hand
now trying to make us all understand

Our nation is at a fork in the road
democracy or dictatorship, the choice we are told

if Trump wins, if he claims victory
you can be sure that is the end of our democracy

So writers and poets have come together
as Writers Against Trump, now and forever

No Biggie

Paranoia or just perception
approaching someone, no mask!
step aside, wait, your reaction.

Why then is it your task
to be the one to acquiesce
Why not say, "Put on your mask!"

People should have more common sense
after all, this is not hard
no reason to be so tense

Getting Covid is just a death card.

Right Before Our Eyes

Humanity can be oblivious
ignoring what is obvious

blinded by desire and greed
failing to grasp the higher need

locked in, reaching for immediacy
unaware they could have the key
to freedom, forever set free.

A House Unsettled

It is a simple compilation
of man-made material
wood, glass, sheet rock, pipes
maybe landscaped for beautification

Then we add items for personalization
maybe a painting or two, photographs,
furniture placed here and there
making the space our own creation

When done there is a realization
that we have created a cliché
a house has now become a home,
we have done our part, contributed to civilization

What is often overlooked in our evaluation
of what makes a house a home
is the energy that pulses within
as a result of the structure's humanization

Each home is unique in this energy distribution
a rhythm is created by the inhabitants within
a predictable pattern emerges as each
life within adds their unique contribution

Quiet, havoc, silence or complete commotion
depending on the pattern of the mindset

and number of inhabitants a home contains
there can be a varied scale of emotions

Regardless of the factors that make up the equation
there is a balance that evolves like weights
on a scale keeping life level and routine
until an outside force causes a change in the
situation

The home that had been a source of relaxation
a place of sanctuary, of stability
no longer peaceful, no longer tranquil
now a place full of anxiety and tension

That which was once a simple compilation
is now a harbinger of complete frustration.

There Is A Difference

Empathy
the ability
to understand and
share the feelings of another

Tragically
not everyone
has this ability
in relating to others

Sympathy
on the other hand
is often confused with
empathy, which is a pity

To pity
or feel sorrow
for the misfortune
of another

unfortunately
is not the same
as sharing the emotion
felt by others

Emotionally
the difference is

more than one of degree
so save your sympathy

It is in no way, empathy.

If Spenser Were Alive Today

Having allowed apathy to prevail
a beast had been released among the town.
An ogre from the worst of fairy tales.
Destruction, division, and even found
to be morally unfit and unsound,
determined to bring about the end of
civilization, to tear everything down
that humanity had now come to love.
Hope that will save us all, must come from above.

Lonesome Blues

I go down to the ocean
and walk along the shore
I go down to the ocean
and walk along the shore
It's sad down at the ocean
cause you ain't here no more

We used to walk together
walking hand in hand
we used to walk together
walking hand in hand
But now I walk alone
only my footprint in the sand

You had me sprinkle your ashes
toss them out to the sea
you had me sprinkle your ashes
toss them out to the sea
One day soon I will join you
when they toss me into the sea.

The Ballade of The Concrete Ship

She was built to fight, built for war
She came too late, never did she
see a battle, now confined offshore.
Towed to Aptos she hoped to be
A gambling Mecca by the sea.
She was gussied up, money spent
to make her glow, invitingly.

She's made of concrete, not cement.

Looking forward they hoped for more.
A resort, tourist destiny
where crowds would gather, folks would pour
in to play, to lose their money.
Nights of dancing so wild and free
but like its name a fallacy.
Mother Nature rose up and meant
her not to be reality.

She's made of concrete not cement.

The waves crashed and the winds did roar
causing a crack so severely
the concrete ship had to close doors
she had to shut permanently

a shell now for eternity.
Lying alone broken and bent
She sits offshore now eerily

She's made of concrete not cement

Birds now make their home in debris
what is left of her now is sent
to sea in pieces, destructively

She's made of concrete not cement.

A Limerick For 45

There once was a flaming narcissist
who refuted the words of the scientists,
his ego and ignorance were rather pathetic
causing thousands to die in the raging pandemic

A New Reality

The ocean never stops
the tide never ceases.
The beach is closed

The sun is shining
but the light is hidden.
Smoke fills the air.

As we pass each other
a nod, a smile not
seen behind the mask

The beach is closed,
smoke fills the air,
we are all wearing masks.

Is this the end?
Or is this the new reality?

A Solo Renku

Fog covers the beach
pelicans diving for fish
autumn is upon us

Inland the sun is blazing
heat rises from the tarmac

Hordes gather, lines form
snakelike, over the hill they
slither to the beach

Chocolate Chips

That which is meant to be
waits unaware of what it may
become only to be molded
by fire into pure ecstasy.

Cigar

Life is very much like a cigar. Or at least a cigar can
be a metaphor for life.
Say cigar, see a cigar, smell the smoke of a cigar and
opinions will fall on one
of two sides. Many react as if it the nastiest habit,
the most obnoxious odor, and
one of the most filthy things one can place in the
mouth. Others, of which I am
one, enjoy the aroma of a fine cigar, sense the
pleasure one receives as nerves calm
with each puff, slowing the world down to a sensible
pace. Holding a cigar in one's hand
makes you think of the labor that created such a
masterpiece. Tightly wound or loosely wrapped,
like people, cigars come in all shapes and sizes. Fat
and thin, long and short, round and square, and
some more pungent than others. Life begins when
we take our first breath and once the umbilical cord
is cut we start out on the road to who knows where.
In the same way a cigar comes to life when fire
meets the end not snipped by the cutter, to begin its
journey of slow elimination. Watching the smoke
rise from a cigar reminds us of how life can be a
meandering series of slowly drifting and finally
dissipating into nothingness.

The Green Stuff

This morning the beach was covered
At least along the shoreline
With a glowing green moss-like substance

A lime green with the texture of zest
Something the high tide had deposited
In the night from the depths of the ocean

Out of the primordial soup my imagination
Told me, an alien presence that was waiting
For the Sun to appear giving it life

Amassing into a huge green monster or
Coagulating into an army of small ones
Gathering in formation to attack at dawn

Charging up the beach to the rental units
Filled with beachgoers unsuspecting their fate
About to become alien cuisine

These were my thoughts as I walked along
Maybe I have read too much Dean Koontz,
But that is a poem for another time.

Chess

Pawn to G-4
Pawn to E-6

There are so many games today
It is hard to decide what to play

There are the old standbys of Monopoly,
Scrabble, Uno, Clue, and Tiddlywinks
But except for Scrabble none make you think

Pawn to F-4
Q to H-4 checkmate

Growing up my dad liked to play Checkers
And I remember he would always win
Whether red or black no difference to him

So, I learned to play chess
a game he never learned
thinking his respect, I might earn

I joined a chess club thinking I was good
Only to lose my first game in four moves
I was playing white and as you can see
It did not take a genius to beat me.

Jail Time

I have never been in prison
I have been at a prison but
Never in one to live, incarcerated

I have been to Alcatraz
And have seen where Capone slept,
And Machine Gun Kelly participated

I have looked out over the bay
To Angel Island where the brothers Anglin
And a guy named Morris were emancipated

Having escaped in the night from Alcatraz
And supposedly swimming to shore
A feat no one had anticipated.

But it was in Walla Walla State Prison
Where I had gone on business
That I was almost humiliated

Walking with a guard, he said
Don't get too close to the wall
An inmate could grab you, unexpected

There are murderers in here
And before you knew what happened
You could find yourself decapitated.

Needless to say, I conducted my business
And very quickly got on my way.

What Day Is It?

I don't really need a calendar
To know what day it is.

If the traffic on our street
Is busy in the morning
It must be a weekday

If the traffic is thin, a Saturday
And if as quiet as after the rapture
It must be Sunday

If the street is lined with bins
Overflowing with discards from my neighbors
It must be Thursday

If before the sun has a chance to appear
And the morning explodes with the sound
Of behemoth trucks banging garbage cans
It must be Friday

I always know it's Monday as I awake
Slightly hung over from Sunday's indulgence
Of too much wine and my one fine cigar

A treat I allow myself as on Sunday afternoon
We sit on the roof deck pondering the meaning of
life

As for Tuesday and Wednesday,
I don't really care which.

Morning Routine

Before the sun breaks the silence of the night, the sound of waves pounding the shore emanates from our CD player, it is 4:20 am.

Sliding out from beneath the warmth of not only the covers, but the heat from my wife's body, I

Slide into a Tee and sweats and move down the hall to grab a can of cat food sitting on a shelve in the laundry room above the cat box, which ironically will be deposited there later.

Stopping at the bottom of the stairs, I stroke the back of the cat at my feet, while the other one darts up the stairs in anticipation of me depositing the food I am carrying

Hitting three switches, the light, the fireplace and the prepared coffee pot I then move to my leather chair waiting for the little beep that says the coffee is ready, as the two cats stare into the fire, still awaiting their food.

The aroma of coffee fills the air and I can't wait for what Anderson Cooper called, "the snap of the brain awakening.," after that first sip.

With coffee at my side I begin my morning meditation that consists of reading (mostly poetry), meditating, and writing my thoughts in a journal.

Once the clock reaches 6 am, it is time to feed the cats and embark on our beach walk, a four-mile round trip along the ocean where the sound of waves pounding the shore is now real.

Each day the sand is shaped anew, each day the sights change. One day dolphins, the next whales. Often a seal or an otter and some days a surprise, like a three-foot Heron standing statuesque.

Back home, I prepare my protein drink and print the daily crossword, my brain food. Did you know that a four-letter word for vivacity is brio? Neither did I.

Once the body and brain have been nourished, I step into to the shower to cleanse the body and refresh the brain. Finally, after dressing, the day begins.

Vive La Différence

As we end our morning walk along the beach
We return home with sand still on our feet
We cross on the flagstones to get to the hose

As I go across, I try not to fall in the lava below
Yes, at seventy-two, this is something I still do
Pretend to be crossing a great divide

My wife sets the nozzle to full
While I change it to jet
She likes it gentle, I like it strong

Is this the difference between
Women and men?

As the day goes by, she gets a new glass
After every third for her water while
I make one last throughout the day

When we heat our leftovers
She likes it lukewarm while
I like it steaming hot

I set mine to cook for 3 to 4 minutes
She sets hers to 2:11 or 2:19
She hates even numbers

Are these the differences between
Women and men?

When I feel it is hot
She says she is cold
A difference, or are we just old?

There a so many things where we are different
But more where we are alike
Not to be cliché, but vive la différence!

I Am Word

If you have read or heard
Paul Selig, who claims to channel
The Divine, you have been exposed
To the phrase, I Am Word

As I pondered this idea of his
I realized, Yes, I Am Word
But I am words, more than one
An idea Mr. Selig seemed to miss

My thoughts consist of words
My voice expresses words
My pen puts down my words
My life is made up of words

Words move from my mind
Out through my pen onto paper
A flow that is natural, unlike
Tapping keys where words are hard to find

Words are how we communicate
With words we tell truth or fabricate
Words are how we each relate
Words describe our life and our fate

So, Mr. Selig, yes , I Am Word
Part of the Divine as you say

But I am also a multitude of words
Making my soul whole, I pray.

Duty

As I open the refrigerator
and grab a carton of milk
I think about all the people
who have never seen a fridge
much less a carton of milk

Pushing a glass against the lever
on the refrigerator door I fill
a glass with water and think
of Flint and how they must
truck in water to survive

Sitting in my chair
with my laptop open
I look at events around the world
struggles, hopelessness, wars
people oppressed and hurting

Then I close my laptop
pickup my crossword and struggle,
hoping to find the four letter word
for responsibility.

The Quandary

The theme is supposed to be ecstasy
Things that bring pleasure to life
But it's hard to ignore what is around me
This country being torn apart, in strife.

Those in power wanting to control, to dominate
Ignoring the hurt, the injustice, the inequality
Stroking the flames of division and hate
They turn their backs on the vast majority.

Blacks die at the hands of the police
To protect and serve a meaningless slogan
Protesters rise up, marching in peace
Only to be met with tear gas and guns.

The coward in charge hides in his bunker
Emerging like a groundhog, Bible in hand
A dictator wannabe, a modern-day Hitler
A buffoon, a clown, none of us can stand.

The question becomes, will things be different?
Is this the moment when a country
wakes up to reality?
Will black lives matter, worth even a cent?
Can hate and bigotry be overcome
by love for humanity?

True North

So there is a sign at our beach
That says a shark was spotted
One half mile north of the end of the pier

Now at the end of the pier is the Concrete Ship
That is famous here and faces directly south
Which would put the shark
in the middle of our street

I wish I had seen this spectacle
Of a shark waddling down the street
Did it greet anyone? Did it stop to say, "Hi?"

Did it stop for ice cream, or did it just pass by?
It could have stopped for pizza, or was it on a mission?
I bet the regulars at the local bar thought
They were seeing a vision.

Now we all know a shark can't walk down the street
So whoever made the sign is someone
I would like to meet

And school them on which direction truly lies
East, West, South and true North.

Curse You Billy Collins

For about 207 days now
I have been ritualistically
Following the ideas put forth
In the Miracle Morning book

Reading for twenty minutes
Meditating for twenty minutes
Journaling and exercising

In the beginning I read self-help books
Then decided if I am a poet
Why not read other poets

Robert Hass, Jorie Graham,
Maddisen Alexandra, and even
Several by Jim Morrison were
My morning fodder of rhyme

Then came Billy Collins
Whom I will refer to as BC

I need to explain that before BC
(pun intended) my meditation
Consisted of me quieting my mind
Entering the realm of the sub conscious

Part of my exercise was to walk the beach

Every morning continuing to meditate
On the wonders of nature
And occasionally having a thought that
Was the seed for a new poem

Then came BC

After beginning my day reading
BC for twenty minutes, my brain
Was exploding with ideas for poems
Of my own. Every line of his seemed
To open a floodgate of words that tumbled
Out of the back of my mind swirling, then
Coalescing into line after line of rhyme.

My beach walk no longer calm
As my brain wrote and rewrote
Word after word all the while
Wishing I had pen and paper.

Reboot

Black lives matter
Blue lives matter
All lives matter
Why not all life matters?

Humans love
Humans hate
Humans dominate
Humans are not all that exist

Supposedly, we were created
In the image of God
How, then, can we not look
At each other and not see Divine

What is it about the makeup of man
That we seek to find difference
Some thing to make us feel superior
Some thing to create divide?

If not race, then religion
If not religion, then geography
If not geography, then technology
If not technology, then position

All may have been created equal
But all were not given opportunity

We all need to learn humility
If ever there is going to be unity

Stars

Every morning
(at least in the spring)
Before the light exchanges
with the dark of night

I find myself as
I sit in my leather chair
looking out through
the octagon window
high above our living room

This time of year
I see two stars
Or maybe one star and Venus
I am not an astronomer

But whatever, one is bright
The other dim telling me
One is closer than the other

As I stare out
I cannot help but think
Of the insignificance of humanity
Meaningless in comparison

We look out and think
We are the center of it all

The universe looks back saying
You humans know nothing at all.

They

The saying
You can't teach an old dog
New tricks, may be true

So, I guess
Although I am old
I am not a dog
I have learned something new

Yes, I learned to say
He, she, madam and sir
Pronouns and nouns to
Reference to whom you refer

Today some now use they
Or zim, sie, em, ter, or ver
Words I have never heard
If it is one person you infer

So, thank you Miss Manners
For clueing me in
With these words that can describe
Both a woman or a man

Faces

The fun part of walking the beach
Every day is seeing the same people
Some we know by name like Chris,
Teresa, Anita, Noreen and her dog Cooper

But most we make up a name
So when we talk about them to
Each other we know who

There is triathlon man and
Glowing lime shirt guy, both
Who run up and down the beach

The old beanie man who always
Flashes the peace sign as we pass
Neanderthal man who stepped out
Of the past, and military man whom
I feel I need to salute

Guard dog couple with a killer on a leash
And Wilson's mom, Wilson being
A small white terrier who is so cute

Then there is garbage bag lady
Who always picks up trash
Creepy guy whose wife always
Walks far behind, maybe needing a break

Tattooed fishing guy who always has
His bike nearby, dog whistle lady who
Can't control her dog, someone needs
To tell her she has the wrong kind of whistle

Camera guy who we haven't seen for a while
Same as the old guy with the old dog
Hope they are all okay

But the most fun is the seal
We see most every day who
Tracks us as we walk along the shore
From the safety of the waves

Early Morning

Clear sky
No wind
Fifty-five degrees
Firm sand
Rolling tide,
Water lapping
On our feet,
Silently a gull
Soars overhead

Then

A dog barking
Owner blows whistle
Calling the dog,
A woman loudly
Talks on a cell,
Drone buzzing
Overhead,
Child screams

Reset
Begin walk
A half hour
Earlier

Clear sky

No wind
Fifty-five degrees
Firm sand
Rolling tide,
Water lapping
On our feet,
Silently a gull
Soars overhead

First Kiss

As our lips meet for the first time
I feel my body dissolve into yours.

As our lips meet for the first time
I lose myself, not sure if I am alive
or in heaven, seduced by an angel.

As our lips meet for the first time
Holding you close, I feel your body
Collapse into mine as your knees go weak.

As our lips meet for the first time
I feel the power of love pulling on
Every fiber of my being.

As our lips meet for the first time
I think of eternity where
There will never be the last.

My Father

As Poncho Villa invaded the U.S.
And General Pershing went after him
My father was born, it was 1916

In the red hills of Carolina, he
Grew up on a farm,
Picking cotton or peanuts,
Drying the peanuts on the barn roof

If his chores were done, he might
Have gone hunting for squirrels
Or down to the creek to fish

His view of the world was mostly
From behind a plow following
A mule, plowing the red fields of Carolina

Oldest of four, a sister and two brothers
He left home at sixteen, lied about
His age and joined the Army-Air Corps

With just a tenth-grade education
He became a success and moved up in rank
Making it a career of twenty-seven years

The year I was born
The Army-Air Corps

Became the Air Force
It was 1947

My father had a warped sense of humor
Was intelligent and harsh, never
Saying I love you. I never measured up

Yet, to this day after he has been long gone
I would still love to hear him say,
"Hey, let's go outside and play catch".

Ecstasy

Ecstasy, if you look, can easily be found.
It can be in a taste, a smell, a vision,
or even a sound.

The taste of a good wine,
Be it red or be it white,
Delights as it passes your lips.
Not too much, or your head will be lite.

The smell of a good meal
On a stove simmering.
Brings a smile to your face,
Leaves your mouth watering.

The sight of a friend or a
Loved one so dear
Makes your heart skip a beat,
Makes you grin ear to ear.

The sound of a song, a tune full of memories.
Lifts the soul, the spirit,
Like sailing across the sea.

Ecstasy, if you look, can easily be found.
It can be in a taste, a smell, a vision,
or even a sound.